BITCOIN

The beginner's guide to mastering bitcoin and digital cryptocurrency – How to Make Money with Bitcoins

Joshua Welsh

Table of Contents

Introduction

INTRODUCTION

Congratulations on downloading this book and thank you for doing so.

The following chapters will discuss simple strategies that you can use to make sure that Bitcoins and Cryptocurrency work for you.

There are plenty of books on this subject on the market, thanks again for choosing this one! Every effort was made to ensure it is full of as much useful information as possible, please enjoy!

CHAPTER 1

WHAT IS BITCOIN?

Bitcoin is the ultimate expression of technological freedom. It is a way for people to pay for different things – both on and off of the Internet – with a currency that does not require the use of a bank or any type of middleman. Bitcoin was created in response to need to have something a little different than the typical bank payment idea and has been successful since the creation.

Creation

In 2009, Bitcoins were created by someone who does not have an actual name. He or she cannot be credited with it because of the alias that was used. It is something that makes it hard to figure out where to direct it to, but the person did it so that they would not get in trouble for making something that is not within regulation for currency.

At its core, Bitcoin is really just a form of trading instead of currency. It is similar to bartering or using things that are not accepted forms of currency to pay for other things. It is a great way for people on the Internet to use something other than money that is connected to a real bank account so that they can make sure that they are safe within the parameters of the Internet.

When Bitcoin was first created, many people did not think that it would catch on or take hold within the online community. It was not worth very much, and people could purchase Bitcoin for pennies on the dollar. It did not have much value at that time. The people who *did* purchase a lot of money's worth of Bitcoin when it first came on the market are the ones who are able to make sure that things are going right now. The Bitcoin is worth a lot more and they are able to cash in on that with both real money and with making purchases using the Bitcoin that they have. They are, essentially, laughing to the bank even though there is no bank involved.

Use

Bitcoins can be used nearly anywhere on the Internet that you would typically use regular currency (like a bank or credit card). There are several major retailers that now accept Bitcoin, and you can make sure that you are able to spend it by first checking with the retailer.

Overstock

The mega-retailer, Overstock, was the first major company on the Internet to first accept Bitcoin. Many other retailers after this started to accept them in the same way so that they are able to cater to people who have Bitcoin. The retail giant has been able to see a lot of success with Bitcoin, and they expect that other companies will follow. They are going to continue accepting Bitcoin for the foreseeable future.

Other Retailers

While it is entirely possible that places like Amazon will start to accept Bitcoin as it grows in popularity, it does not currently accept it. The nice part, though, is that people can still use their Bitcoin on Amazon. There is one site that has set up a special program for people who have Bitcoin, Gyft. This is a site that deals exclusively in gift cards, and you can purchase the gift cards by using Bitcoin. You can buy gift cards at places like Walmart, Amazon and other retailers. You can even buy physical gift cards instead of just the codes so that they are delivered to you, and you can use them in an actual store as opposed to just online.

Physical Locations

While there are not many locations that will accept Bitcoin as payment right now, there are still some locations that will take Bitcoin as payment. There is a major jewelry retailer, Reed's, that does accept Bitcoin in the physical stores and some one-off retailers that will accept Bitcoins as payment. It is expected that, in the future, you will be able to buy everything from your groceries to manicures with the Bitcoin that you have accumulated online.

Safety

Using Bitcoin is one of the safest options that is available on the Internet. While there is not much security when it comes to viruses on your computer and accidental deletion of the Bitcoin that you have stored in your virtual wallet, it is still much safer than trying to use a bank to keep all of your money.

One of the biggest points of safety is that you do not have to worry about whether or not the money is going to go away because the bank is closing or there is an issue with the insurance on the bank. You can have millions in Bitcoin and not have to worry about the FDIC or being subjected to taxes on the Bitcoin because they are not considered currency. They are something that you own and something that you can trade to make sure that you get the most out of the situation.

It is worth noting that Bitcoin is also a relatively sound investment. When Bitcoins were first available on the market, it was not worth nearly as much as what it currently is. The price for Bitcoin was low, and it was something that people did not think was going to take off. In a surprising twist, Bitcoin surged in price, and they were able to make a lot of people a lot of money. It was something that they had and something that they were able to increase in value. Since that point, Bitcoin has increased in value. At one point, it was worth as much as what gold is worth.

Anonymity

One of the biggest positive points of using Bitcoin is the anonymity that comes with using it. You do not need to give any personal information, you don't need to open a bank account, and your Bitcoin will never even be attached to your own name. It will all be done through the ID number that is attached to your "wallet" that is all virtual, and it is something that will never have your name hooked up to it.

If you want to buy or sell something or even trade Bitcoin with other people, they won't ever have to know your name. This is great if you make a lot of online transactions and if you want to stay anonymous. While many people who do illegal activity online enjoy the anonymity, there are plenty of legitimate reasons that people may want to stay anonymous while they are online.

Even though there is no way to trace the Bitcoin back to your name, your location or anything that identifies you, there is still a log of what has been purchased and sold with Bitcoin. It is important to note that this log will track everything that goes on with Bitcoin, the unique IDs that come with the wallets and the actual information of the specific Bitcoins. By looking at this information, you can see the past purchases you have made and the people who you have worked with in the past. You may not know their names, but you can see their IDs from the purchases that you have made with the Bitcoin.

Unique

Each Bitcoin has a unique identifier to it. This is something that protects the Bitcoin as well as the users. Since each one is different and they are encrypted with their own codes, people cannot just make their own Bitcoin. It is something that will allow them to make sure that they are getting real Bitcoin and that it is not counterfeit. Since each one has their own code, that is how they are traced to different transactions and how they can be bought and sold.

Along with the fact that the individual Bitcoins have their own unique identifiers, the wallets of the people who buy and sell Bitcoin also have their own unique codes. This is something that allows them to trade, buy and sell. There are many different things that users can do with Bitcoins, but it is all done from their wallet. The wallet is never actually attached to the person or the person's identifiable information, but it can be traced over different transactions. The wallet ID number can be connected to an email if the user wishes.

There are many different applications that can be used both on smartphones and computers that allow users to trade the Bitcoin and sell things using their

Bitcoin. These apps require only that the person has their wallet ID. As long as they have Bitcoin within that wallet, they will be able to make sure that they are paying for different things. The unique identification of each of the Bitcoin in the wallet in combination with the wallet identification number will allow the user to be identified and verified to make purchases. There needs to be enough Bitcoin in a user's virtual wallet to be able to make purchases or to even consider using the Bitcoin.

CHAPTER 2

MASTERING BITCOIN

There is not much to mastering Bitcoin. It is similar to any other investment that you can make in that it rises and falls in price. There are different limits on it, and you can use it just like you would use a typical currency. This section will tell you the different specifics of Bitcoin and how it can be used. While Bitcoin is much different from other currency forms, it is not much different from the other types of investments that you can make, like gold or silver.

Buying It

There are several different options when it comes to buying Bitcoin. When you are first getting started, you need to buy it from an authorized seller. This is often a site that takes some information from you and allows you to either purchase the Bitcoin from your bank account or using a debit or credit card. The site (that also often has an application for your cell phone) will then be the place where you do everything from. It is where the "home" of your wallet will be and where you can make sure that you have all of your Bitcoin stored at.

The most popular sites, like Coinbase, allow you to store your Bitcoin in the cloud. This helps to keep yours from accidentally deleting them or from any virus that could get onto your computer that could harm them. It is important to note that these sites are *not* banks and they do not guarantee that your Bitcoin will be safe – only that you will have a place to buy and sell them from.

They are responsible for where you can exchange real money for Bitcoin and where you can make sure that you are doing things the right way with your Bitcoin.

Selling Bitcoin

Selling your Bitcoin is as easy as giving it back to the

site that you originally got it from. You can exchange it back for cash, and the money will either go back onto your debit or credit card, or it will go back into your bank. The reason that people sell their Bitcoin is to make money, so you want to make sure that you are selling it at the right time to avoid losing money on it. Keep an eye on the price of the Bitcoin so that you know when to sell it.

The risk that you take when you have Bitcoin is that the price will drop too far below what you paid for it. While the price has steadily risen in the past, that does not mean that it is going to rise for the rest of time. It is important to note that you will not be able to make money off of the Bitcoin if it drops. Buying and selling *any* type of investment involves some level of risk so you should make sure that you are truly prepared to sell the Bitcoin.

Using It

When you are online, you can use Bitcoin to buy things just like you would with a typical form of payment. While you can't exactly buy things like a house with Bitcoin right now, you can cash the Bitcoin in (and pay an exchange rate), or you can invest in gift cards to use in real life situations.

The positive part of Bitcoin is that it is not much you can't buy online. With the world in a technological craze, you can buy everything from vehicles to beauty services online. All you need is a site that accepts Bitcoin or a gift card that you purchased with Bitcoin.

Investing in It

Bitcoin is a great investment no matter what you are hoping to get out of it. The trends for Bitcoin are great, and the yield is expected to be much higher than what it was in the past. Bitcoin is nearly the same price as gold and will continue to rise. It is expected to surge past gold. Some financial professionals have even predicted that one Bitcoin will be worth $10,000 or more in the coming years. That is not a bad price for something that started below one cent per Bitcoin.

When Bitcoin was first started in 2009, people were not impressed with it. They did not think that it would catch on and the price for each Bitcoin was very low. The few people who were *not* skeptical did invest some money in it. One of the most popular cases was a person who invested 27 dollars in the Bitcoin when it first came on the market. That equaled about 5,000 Bitcoin. The buyer forgot about them until 2013 when the prices were extremely high for Bitcoin. He checked the Bitcoin that he had with the prices that were listed on the Bitcoin, and it ended up that he had just under 1 million dollars worth of Bitcoin. If he had waited until 2017 to cash in on the Bitcoin, he would have had 5 million dollars. His investment of 27 dollars was a low-risk investment that ended up having a huge reward in the end.

In the short time that Bitcoin has been available as a trade option, it has increased by thousands of times. It has gone from being worth less than one cent to being worth right around 1,000 dollars per Bitcoin. People who purchased Bitcoins at the beginning of the period that they were available are now cashing in on millions of dollars for the small purchases that they made less than 10 years ago.

Fluctuation

If you look at any type of investment, you can see that there is a major fluctuation from hour to an hour and even from minute to minute. As an example, while writing the previous section about investing, the price of Bitcoin was at $933.15 per Bitcoin. While this section is being written, it is down to $928.44. By the time that the next section is written, the Bitcoin price will probably change again. As with any type of investment, you need to be careful about how closely you watch the fluctuation. If you watch it on a regular basis, you can see if there is a major spike or dip (the point at which you would sell or buy, respectively) in the price of Bitcoin. Watching it faithfully will often allow you the chance to cash in on a glitch or a random dip in the price. It is not uncommon for it to dip as low as $100 for a few minutes but it can also spike as high as $3,000 for a few minutes. If you are watching it closely, you can see those and buy when it is $100 just to turn around and sell it when it is $3,000.

The problem with watching all of the time is that you can become obsessive about it. You may get excited over minor spikes or dips which could cause you to lose money on the Bitcoin if you are buying or selling it. This can be a problem for the Bitcoin that you already have in your possession, too, because it will change the value of the Bitcoin.

Rising Prices

Even though there is a lot of fluctuation that goes on during an hourly basis and even from day to day, Bitcoin, for the most part, has been rising since the day it was first introduced to the online market. This is something that has allowed it to be even better than most investment options. While the prices of gold and silver have gone down and may not even be worth as much as what they were 15 years ago, Bitcoin has increased in a time that is short. In less than a decade, Bitcoin has seen a rise in value each year that it has been on the market.

The rising prices are good for Bitcoin and even better for people who use it. As it rises in price, more people are buying into it to try to get some of the great returns that people have already seen. Since it is becoming increasingly popular, more locations are accepting it as a form of currency which has allowed to become even more popular. It is a constant cycle of the rising value and the ability of people to use it.

Finding It

While the most common way to get Bitcoin is buying it and trading it on the exchange and for different products, there are also other ways that people can get Bitcoin. This is similar to gold in that it is able to be "mined." People are not rushing to Northern California, though, to find it like they did with the gold rush. Instead, they are flocking to websites that have Bitcoin up for grabs and that people must constantly try to find the codes for. Once they find the encryption, the Bitcoin is theirs to keep.

In the past, finding Bitcoin was much easier because not as many people knew about it. The popularity of Bitcoin is a double-edged sword though when it comes to mining. Now that more people know about the ability to mine Bitcoin, they are doing it, and the reserves of the currency are running out making it harder for people to find it. Some people have even set up their mining process to be professional, and people do it for the sole purpose of trying to find it. They are professional miners and those who work hard to make sure that they find it. They have dedicated all of their time working to mining Bitcoin.

Organic Bitcoin

Even though Bitcoin isn't necessarily organic in the way that gold would be, it still occurs on websites and in certain situations naturally. These are Bitcoins that have been encrypted to be hidden, and the creators of the currency have left them in places on the Internet for people to find. They are the same as Bitcoin that have been purchased or exchanged for goods and services, and they can be used in the same way as those are. As soon as someone finds and organic Bitcoin, they are able to put it in their wallet just like they would with one that they got through a different method.

It is not quite as easy as going out with a pickaxe and looking around for Bitcoin, though. The process is somewhat complicated and will be found in the next chapter but, in essence, Bitcoin mining involves solving complicated algorithms and putting them into practice for Bitcoin in exchange. It is a win-win situation for the miner and the creator of the Bitcoin. They are able to get their problems solved while the miner is able to make money.

Keeping It

One of the best things that Bitcoin owners can do with their Bitcoin is hanging onto it and keep it safe in their wallet. When someone purchases Bitcoin, they should not think of it as just another form of cash that they can spend on the Internet. Doing this causes it to be not as valuable and can create problems for them if the price continues to rise. It can be complicated to understand but losing out on Bitcoin will make things harder on the wallet owner.

If someone has Bitcoin and keeps it in their virtual wallet, they will be able to make more money of it. It is a good idea for someone who has a lot of Bitcoin to think of it as a stock or another type of investment that they have made. If you buy up 10 bars of gold, you would probably hold onto them until they are more valuable instead of trying to pay for a new set of ear buds that you think you might want from a Chinese retailer.

Think of your Bitcoin as an investment instead of currency and you will be able to cash in on the higher price of Bitcoin in the future if you hold onto it.

CHAPTER 3

MINING BITCOIN

Perhaps one of the most complicated parts of understanding Bitcoin is understanding where it comes from and how it is created: mining. This is the process by which people are able to get Bitcoin in a way that does not involve buying, trading or selling. It is organic, and they are able to get Bitcoins for doing certain tasks. The way that Bitcoin mining works benefits both the person who is doing the mining as well as the Bitcoin community where the mining prospects are coming from in the different areas that the coins can be found at.

The Miner

The most important part of Bitcoin mining is the miner who is looking for Bitcoin. This is the person who searches to find the Bitcoin and who can make sure that the problems get solved to be able to get to the Bitcoin. It is an important job and something that is necessary for people to be able to do. There are many miners, but only a few of them do it on a full-time basis that will allow them the chance to make things better in their community. They can mine for different reasons, but the biggest reason is to get more Bitcoin instead of having to trade and sell things for them.

When a miner is first getting started, he or she usually learns from someone else who mines. This person shows the future miner the "ropes" of looking for Bitcoin and solving the problems to make sure that they are getting Bitcoin. The miner needs to learn the ins and outs including the right way to solve problems, how to understand a legitimate purchase and the right way to make things work within the Bitcoin community.

It is not a bad idea for people want to get into Bitcoin mining to get started with buying, trading and selling first. They can learn the right way to handle their

Bitcoin which will give them a better chance at making sure they know what a legitimate transaction looks like when they are doing different things in the mining community.

While Bitcoin mining can help people to get more Bitcoin, it is something that does require work. You can't just sit back and expect to find the Bitcoin for free when you are trying to mine it – you must work for it.

Community Help

The Bitcoin community came up with the idea for mining in response to a problem. After Bitcoin had increased in value, not everyone was able to afford them, and the community felt that there needed to be a way for people to be able to get them without having to spend a lot of money on them. This was something that was important to the community, and they wanted others to make sure that they were able to get the Bitcoin that they desired. They saw it as a problem.

The other problem that the community had been falsified transactions. When Bitcoin first came on the market, people could, essentially, reuse the same Bitcoin over and over again. Since they did not want to be connected to banks, there was no paper trail or any type of record that was attached to the Bitcoin. People took advantage of that, and it made a lot of false transactions for the Bitcoin and made it harder for people to make sure that they were getting a true Bitcoin. There were a few problems that stemmed from this initial problem and the community wanted to make sure that it did not go any further than what was happening with it.

The solution that they had to both of these problems was simple: Bitcoin mining. People could solve problems that they had with the Bitcoin and be able to earn Bitcoin from doing it. It was a bit like a job and something that they felt that they had to work to earn money for. It made sense, though, that people could do that. They were able to see the problems, or the trails that followed the Bitcoin, and make sure that they were legitimate transactions. In exchange for approving (or denying) the transaction, they were rewarded with Bitcoin that they could add to their own wallet.

Starting Bitcoin mining cut down on the fraudulent transactions and the ability of people to duplicate transactions with Bitcoin. Every Bitcoin that is spent goes through a miner who makes sure that it is not one that has already been spent somewhere else. The miner works to make sure that the trail is accurate and that any information that is added to it is done so in a way that makes sense. This does not even take extra time and is so seamless that most people don't even realize when their Bitcoin has gone through a miner.

Hardware

While anyone is able to become a miner, it does take some special software to be able to do it in a way that is quick and efficient (which is the goal of all miners). The miners need to first learn the ropes from an experienced miner or on their own (which can be difficult). They then need to get a certain type of hardware to be able to run the numbers and do the algorithms by which the Bitcoins are spent, exchanged and traded.

The Raspberry Pi collection is one of the most popular hardware devices that you can use to make sure that you have the right equipment to be able to mine Bitcoin. It is a good idea to use this and to set it up in a way that will allow you the chance to make your own math problems and to solve them in the right way. By using the Raspberry Pi, you can set it up to do what you want. It functions as a hard drive, and it will work in combination with any monitor that you have.

Since it can be complicated to build your own system, you should try to get plans to build your mining device. This is something that you can do by doing the right amount of research or by using one that was created by a different miner. The person who you have chosen to follow and learn about mining from will be able to give you an idea of what you need to use to be able to make your Raspberry Pi work for you. Using premade plans can help you create it in a way that works for Bitcoin mining.

Another option would be to purchase a completely done system for Bitcoin mining. It is something that you can purchase from Bitcoin mining sites and something that will allow you the chance to make sure that you can do things the right way when it comes to mining. Always making sure that you are doing things the right way with mining can all be done from the system and will be a way for you to increase the amount of mining that you can do. When you purchase a system that is already created, like the Avalon6, you will be able to save the time that it would normally take you to build your own machine.

Collecting on Bitcoin

Once you have done the math problems and approved or denied the transaction with Bitcoin, you will be able to collect on the Bitcoin that the community owes to you for making sure that you can do things the right way with mining. Always making sure that you have the right equipment is the best way to make things better for Bitcoin mining but collecting on the money that you have earned is important, too. It is a good idea to do as many as you can so that you will be able to make as much money as possible. You can earn more money with the more transactions that you look at and approve, and you will be able to add more Bitcoin to your wallet each time that you do it.

It is an automatic process that is done as soon as you solve the problem and take a look at the trail. Once you have approved it, you will need to enter in your wallet ID, and the Bitcoin will be put into your wallet. This transaction, ironically, will be sent to another miner who will be able to approve it since it is a legitimate one.

As you begin to mine, you will find that it takes less time for you to make the decisions on transactions in the community. Not only will that help the people who are making the transactions because they will be able to go through more quickly but it will help you too. The more transactions that you approve in a certain amount of time, the more Bitcoin you will be able to make and collect in your wallet. It is always a good idea to make sure that you are collecting on all of the Bitcoin possible.

The more that you mine, the better you will get. The better you get at mining, the less it will take you to make decisions. The quicker you make decisions, the more money you will be able to make in each of some times that it takes you to be able to do that. As long as you are always getting faster at approving transactions, you will be able to make more money per hour from Bitcoin mining. This will allow you to increase all of the Bitcoin that you have and the money that you are able to make with it.

Making Mining Happen

After you have decided that you are going to be a Bitcoin miner, you need to get started as quickly as possible. The sooner you start, the sooner you can make money from it. There are several steps to getting started, but once you have done these, you will be able to make Bitcoin. The amount of Bitcoin that you can make is limited only by your speed and your ability to make more money when you are in different situations. It can be harder for you to make the right amount of money if you do not know what you are doing with Bitcoin so always try your hardest to get started as quickly as possible.

When you make the decision to mine Bitcoin, you should find someone who already does it. This person will be your mentor and will be the reason that you are able to make money and figure out everything that there is to mining. You should take your time and select the right person for the job – someone who is knowledgeable and can teach you the things that you want to know about mining.

Once you have done all of this, you are ready to get started. Make sure that your software is ready and get out there to mine Bitcoin. You will be able to truly start making money from it. The best part about mining Bitcoin is that you will eventually be able to replace a full-time job with it. This will give you the chance to do more with your time and can even give you more free time. It is a way to work from home and as your own boss.

Some of the best Bitcoin miners can make upwards of $1,000 per day finding around 1 Bitcoin per day or more. These are the people who are making the most money from it. The bonus comes in the fact that the Bitcoin are still growing in value. For example, someone who was Bitcoin mining three years ago for 10 days in a row and got 10 Bitcoins now has 10 Bitcoins that are worth around $10,000 total. They were not worth that much when that person was mining, and they have gone up in value. It is like automatically investing the money that you make at your "job."

CHAPTER 4

TRADING BITCOIN

There are many different ways that you can trade Bitcoin. You can trade it for goods, services, for other currencies and even with different Bitcoin. Trading Bitcoin is similar to trading any other type of investment and may result in you making more money than what you could with other investments. Because of the way that Bitcoin works, you do not need to work hard to be able to trade it the right way.

Services

When someone performs services for someone online or in a different medium, there are many ways that the person can be paid for the service. One of the ways that are becoming increasingly popular is Bitcoin. If you do a service for someone, you may request to be paid in Bitcoin.

While this is something that is still relatively unknown and not widely used, it is more common on the Internet. If you are doing the service online, the chances are higher that the person would be willing to pay for it in Bitcoin than it would be to pay for it in another way. It is important to note that people may want to be paid for their services in Bitcoin because they are able to make more money from the Bitcoin than they would with a more traditional form of payment.

If you are doing a physical service instead of an online service, it may be less likely that you can be paid in Bitcoin. Both parties need to own Bitcoin to be able to do this, and both must have their own wallet. In some instances, it is just easier to be paid in cash and to purchase the Bitcoin with the cash that you have made. This will allow you to improve on the Bitcoin.

This is just one of the ways that Bitcoin is traded on the Internet. Since they are not officially recognized as currency, it is more of a trade than a payment. You own the Bitcoin, and you can trade someone for the services. There are many different services that will allow you to trade Bitcoin for them and you can even offer *your* services for Bitcoin. It is not a bad idea to do this because the Bitcoin will be much more valuable than getting paid on the dollar.

Goods

Goods are offered similarly to services when it comes to Bitcoin. When someone has a good to offer, they can offer to sell it for either traditional forms of payment or Bitcoin. When they choose Bitcoin, they are going to get paid more than if they were getting paid in cash. There are many options that come along with Bitcoin payments, but the best ones are the ones that allow the buyer to pay in Bitcoin for something that is worth more than what they have paid for.

People will sometimes offer different payment options for people who are paying with Bitcoin because of the higher value of Bitcoin. This means that you can make sure that you are getting the most out of the Bitcoin when you are trying to sell things, and you can get more for what you are paying for. Sellers will offer this option because they know that the Bitcoin is not only worth more right when it is being used but that it will also grow in value over the time that the person has it. The longer that they keep the Bitcoin in their wallet, the more it will be worth for them in the future.

It is important to note that not all goods can be sold for Bitcoin. Sites like Etsy and other creation sites allow people to purchase in Bitcoin, but not every site will allow that. Small businesses benefit from this because they will be able to grow the money that they have made in profit but it is important to note that not all small businesses, especially those that are new, will be able to offer payment options in Bitcoin. It is just not on the radar for these businesses right now, but it is expected to become a more popular option in the future.

Traditional

Since Bitcoin can be handled in the same way that other trading options, like stocks, are, they are easy for people to trade in a traditional sense. If you have Bitcoin, you can trade them in the same way that you would trade other types of currency and things like stocks. While they are not necessarily on the stock market, you can use the same principles that come along with the market to be able to trade your Bitcoins.

It is a good idea to make sure that you have a decent amount of Bitcoin before you start to trade them in a traditional sense. In general, you should have around 10 Bitcoin (or close to $10,000 worth of them) before you make the decision to start trading them. If you only have one Bitcoin and you try to trade it, you will need to divide it into different parts which are great for buying and selling but may make things more complicated for you when you are trading the Bitcoin.

While it is not necessarily a problem to break your Bitcoin apart to be able to trade it, it may make things more complicated for you. It can be messy and make you have dividends that are not even. You should make sure that you have enough Bitcoin to be able to trade before you make the decision to do so. There are many options when it comes to adding more Bitcoin to your wallet but always making sure that you have more than enough for trading is the only way that you can truly be successful with trading.

One thing that you need to keep in mind all of the time when you are trading Bitcoin is that you need to make sure that you are getting the most out of the situation and that you should always trade up. Make sure that the value of your Bitcoin is high and that you are able to get more Bitcoin than what you initially had. If you do not do this, you may lose out on money and not be able to take full advantage of the trades that you have.

The point of traditional trading is to grow the amount of money that you have in Bitcoin just from moving it around, buying it and selling it for large margins and great returns.

Buying

When you are buying Bitcoin, you should make sure that you are paying the lowest price possible for the Bitcoin. Keep an eye on the price to figure out what the return is going to be. If you look at the past of the prices, you can see what the yields will be on the Bitcoin and accurately predict it so that it will make more sense for you to be able to buy it. The lower the price that you can get the Bitcoin for, the better the return will be and the more money you will be able to make off of the Bitcoin.

If you notice that the trends are going in one way or another, try to buy your Bitcoin at that time. You should always buy it when it is as low as possible and make sure that you have enough money to be able to buy as many as possible. If you buy 3 Bitcoin at one time, you will have those three to be able to keep in your wallet and save up for later on. If you look at the Bitcoin trends from the past, you can see that Bitcoin has grown exponentially over the past eight years. They have jumped from less than one cent per unit to over 1,000 dollars per unit. If you buy them for 1,000 dollars, you are not going to get as good as a deal as those who paid less than one cent, but if the price rises to 10,000 dollars per unit or more, you will be able to enjoy the return that comes from the Bitcoin.

The chances are that your Bitcoin price will rise significantly over the next 12-24 months and you will be able to cash in on the investment that you have made.

Selling

Opposite from the way that buying works, you need to sell your Bitcoin or exchange it for real money, when it is at the highest point. Throughout the day, there will be many high points, but you need to watch for the highest point within a term or a quarter. This is the point at which you will be able to make the most amount of money, and it is important that you are truly able to profit off of the money that you make from the Bitcoin.

You can figure out when the Bitcoin is going to be at

its highest by looking, again, at the trends. There are different trends that will make things worth it and will make you better able to do more with the Bitcoin that you have. Each of these trends can change the time that you are going to sell your Bitcoin.

Looking at the trends will give you an idea of what the Bitcoin is going to yield for you. Since the yield amount is often higher than the return on the Bitcoin, you should be careful about when you sell the Bitcoin. It is always a good idea to make sure that you are doing the most when it comes to your Bitcoin. Try your hardest to maintain all of the money that you have and sell the Bitcoin for the highest amount.

One thing that you can do is watch the Bitcoin market for an entire day. Look at the different trends and see at which point it is at its highest. This will generally be a few hours before the opening of the day or a few hours after the day has closed. Even though the day fluctuates, you can still sell after it has closed.

It is also a good idea to hold onto the Bitcoin for as long as possible. You do not want to do too much trading so that you can keep as much money as possible. Since Bitcoin nearly always rise in price, you will be able to make more money the longer that you hold onto them for.

Trades

The point of buying and selling Bitcoin is to get the highest trade amount possible. Different trade amounts will be different depending on how much you have accumulated in Bitcoin, but you should know that the more that you trade, the lower the chances of being able to make a lot of money off of the Bitcoin will be. Try to hang onto it for as long as possible.

If you know the right time to buy Bitcoin and you take advantage of it in every way possible, you will be able to make a lot of money from Bitcoin. If you consider the people who purchased Bitcoin in 2009 and are still holding onto it in 2017, you can see that they are clearly the ones who have made a lot of profit from it. Selling it and rebuying it is not in your best interest when it comes to Bitcoin even though it may be a good idea for other investments that you have made or that you are going to make.

The time will come that you need to get rid of your Bitcoin. Keep an eye out for the right time to be able to sell it. It is a good idea to try to hang onto it for as long as possible but selling it can truly have its benefits. If you think of the people who bought hundreds of dollars worth of Bitcoin in 2009, you can see that they are now able to sell it for millions of dollars.

CHAPTER 5

VALUE OF BITCOIN

The value of Bitcoin has been steadily rising since they were first introduced to the market in 2009. Since they were just a concept idea and something that not many people knew about, they were not worth a lot at that time. While they are still relatively unknown, they have risen in price by thousands of times. As they continue to grow in popularity, it is expected to continue to rise in value. The outlook for Bitcoin is good as long as people continue to learn more about it.

The prices that are reflected below are reflective of the average summer value of Bitcoin except for the year of 2017 where there is only data from the month of January.

2009

The price of Bitcoin was around .0001 USD.

This is the value of the Bitcoin and where it started at. This was the point of which they were the least popular because they had just made their appearance on the market. People were somewhat skeptical about the Bitcoin, but some people chose to invest in them at this point.

The creator of Bitcoin invested in the most and is still considered to have the largest Bitcoin wallet out of everyone in the world. The United States FBI also purchased their wallet full of Bitcoin at this point just in case it was to rise in value.

Anyone who purchased Bitcoin in 2009 began to see returns on it almost immediately. Two years after their initial investment in the Bitcoin, they would have a huge return on it. It is something that many people could not have anticipated, but the people who did make the investment are now very wealthy. Since they were worth *so* little in 2009, it would not have cost a lot of money to make an investment that would change their lives. For as little as $25, someone could have purchased 250,000 Bitcoin. Two years later, that $25 worth would have been equal to around $3.75 million.

2010

The price of Bitcoin was around .07 USD.

Even though it has only been on the market for one year, this was a major turning point for Bitcoin and the price that they were set at. It was 700 times the amount that they came onto the market at only 12 months before. It was one of the largest and fastest returns that anyone had seen in any market in the history of trading.

People who had not been paying attention to Bitcoin or who were still leery of what Bitcoin was (or how it would perform) began to shift their attention to Bitcoin. Much more people began investing in it at this point and, at the same time, it began to be a regular "currency" that was used online.

The cost for each unit of Bitcoin was still relatively low compared to some of the other shares that were found on the market, and this was something that people could clearly see when they were buying it. If someone purchased around $25 worth of Bitcoin in 2010, they would get about 350 units of Bitcoin. One year later, this $25 worth would be worth $5,250.

As more people caught onto the fact that Bitcoin was really going to be something worth investing in, the value of Bitcoin began to rise...very quickly.

2011

The price of Bitcoin was 15 USD.

The need to buy more Bitcoin and the demand that was brought about by investors caused the price to skyrocket from the second year into the third. Thousands of people were pushing for thousands of shares in Bitcoin, and this was something that they knew was going to take off. It was a huge increase of money that the Bitcoin was worth and was the first time that it was able to rise about the one dollar mark.

This was the first time that Bitcoin mining really became a popular thing. While it had always been a possibility, it was not something that people really thought to do and was not the most popular option. People who wanted to get a lot more Bitcoin were able to mine it. One of the biggest miners and most popular miners was actually the person who invented it, and that holds true still in this day and age.

It rose so far beyond one dollar that it actually made it all the way up to 15 dollars. People began clamoring for Bitcoin but what they did not know was that the supply of it was going to increase too. While the demand began to rise, so did the supply and that caused some issues with the value.

2012

The price of Bitcoin was 7 USD.

In 2012, Bitcoin took a huge hit from the point that it was just one year before. This was the first time that Bitcoin had gone down in value and it was probably because people did not see them as valuable any longer. There was enough Bitcoin to meet the demands of people who were hoping to invest their money in different things, and it was something that they knew that they needed to be able to get.

When people began to see that they could get as many Bitcoin as they wanted simply by purchasing them, it drove the value down.

Any good investor knows, though, that there is usually a slight downturn in the value of an investment before there is a major uptick in it. This is something that happens with nearly any type of investment opportunity, including stocks. People who invest know that there are a lot of things that they can do to make sure that they are keeping up with the price and that they are getting the most for their money.

2013

The price of Bitcoin was 100 USD.

After the downturn that happened in 2013, it came as

somewhat of a surprise for people to see that the Bitcoin surged up to 100 USD. What came as an even bigger surprise was the fact that, at one point during 2013, the Bitcoin price reached all the way up to $1,200 per unit. This was both the first time that it rose about $100 and the first time that it rose about $1,000. It showed that the year before was a one-off year and something that was not going to happen again in the way that different things would be able to go on with Bitcoin.

The $100 price stood at the average for that year, and it ended up that it would likely be another two years before the price would reach that $1,200 mark again.

The huge uptick, though, caused another wave of investors to purchase more Bitcoin.

It is also important to note that 2013 was the year that the Silk Road was shut down and millions of dollars worth of Bitcoin that had been held by illegal dealers were sold off or auctioned off. During this time, the FBI acquired a huge portion of Bitcoin which put them as one of the biggest stakeholders.

They are among the *only* Bitcoin owners that are known in the top 10% because they have publicly announced it. The rest may own more than them, but they have chosen complete anonymity that is offered by Bitcoin.

2014

The price of Bitcoin was 600 USD.

As more people began investing in Bitcoin, the price continued to rise. This was something that was expected during that year, but people began to see that their Bitcoin investments were going to pay off. Those who had purchased $25 worth of Bitcoin in 2009 and had held onto it since that time could cash that in for a smooth $150 million dollars. This was a huge return on an investment of only $25. The return was millions of the original percentage of what they had invested.

Not many people were able to hold onto their money until that point, but the ones who did were wise to continue hanging onto it because the next two years would prove to be *very* profitable. As more people began to see how much the Bitcoin really cost, they began to back off and not as many people meant that there would be another downturn in the market value of the Bitcoin.

2015

The price of Bitcoin was 220 USD.

This was in sharp contrast to the huge rise that was seen in 2014. It was something that people did not see coming, and people began to clamor around to make sure that they were selling them so that they were able to profit. With more Silk Roaders on trial, people began to sell off their Bitcoin hoping that they would still be able to make a profit. While this *was* a low point for Bitcoin, the people who chose to continue holding onto their Bitcoin despite the market downturn were the ones who would be able to profit in the long run.

Despite the fact that the $220 price was a low point for Bitcoin, 2015 was the second year that people would see Bitcoin rise up to $1,200. When it hit that point toward the end of 2015, it did not go back down to the $220 price point nad continued to fluctuate within $300 of $1,000. The low point was around $700 while the highest point was $1,300.

2015 was the year that Bitcoin truly became worth its (nonexistent) weight in gold.

2016

The price of Bitcoin was $1,146.

Since the price began to rise in 2015 and stayed there throughout the year and into 2016, people began to cash in on their Bitcoin payments. They knew that it was going to be a good time to sell off the money that they had acquired in Bitcoin and they wanted to be able to make as much money as possible from Bitcoin. Since most things that are involved in investing are measured in comparison to gold, they figured since the Bitcoin was worth the same as (and sometimes more than) gold, that would be the time to let it go.

In 2014, a major investment estimator guessed that by 2018, Bitcoin would be worth $10,000 per unit. This was a long way off from what it was in 2016, but there is still a 2-year difference in the two. The exponentials are not expected to increase that much anymore, but anything is possible with Bitcoin since it is in a free market and is subject to nearly anything. The 2016 United States presidential election could have a major impact on the way that Bitcoin is treated but only time will tell.

2017

At the time that this book was written, Bitcoin sat at $922 per unit.

This is on the low end of the past 12-month average but is still a good number compared to the original .0001 price that Bitcoin was originally worth. With all of the new political changes that are coming to the United States, there is expected to be a change in the Bitcoin. Whether that is for the good or the bad of Bitcoin is left to be determined.

Professional investors, algorithm makers, and yield hopefuls are still predicting that the Bitcoin will continue to rise. There is expected to be a surge in the economy, and that can have a great positive effect on the free market. While it is unlikely that the Bitcoin will be worth $10,000 by 2018, there is still going to be a major change in Bitcoin. Anyone who wants in on the game should do so in 2017 because the prices if based on the trends are going to keep going up.

While it is entirely possible that the price of Bitcoin may drop for a short time (based off of the past trends), there is a good chance that it will have a huge increase after that initial drop down.

CHAPTER 6

MAKING MONEY

The point of getting Bitcoin and spending all of the efforts on learning about it is to make money from it, right? There are many options when it comes to making money, and there isn't a single way that is better than the other ways to be able to make money but you need to decide which way is going to be the best for you to make money so that you will be doing the right thing with the Bitcoin that you have (or the Bitcoin that you *want* to have).

If you look at each of these ideas and do not find one that works for you, Bitcoin investing may not be your best option, and you may want to consider putting your investment money into something else instead of wasting your time trying to make money from Bitcoin.

Mining

Many people think that mining is the key to being able to make a lot of Bitcoin. They think this because they do not believe that they are going to have to spend any money to be able to make the Bitcoin that they want. The biggest problem with that is that they *do* have to spend money and it is often much more than what they would be able to just buy the Bitcoins with and wait for them to become mature when it comes to different types of currency.

Bitcoin mining is not worth it for people who only mine a few Bitcoin and then quit. The only money that is to be had in mining is for people who mine a large number of Bitcoin at one time. This is something that they need to have the right equipment and the time to invest in. It is a big part of the way that things are done in mining, and there are many different things that can make up the Bitcoin mining experience.

The equipment alone can cost thousands of dollars and may only result in a person getting a few coins from the mining process. Even if they *do* have the right equipment and get it done the right way, they may not be able to make the coins. Instead of spending tens of thousands of dollars, they can put that money into buying actual Bitcoin from reputable sources, holding onto them and selling them for huge profits later on.

One of the biggest problems with mining is not even knowing whether you are going to get the Bitcoins as a result. You may not be able to mine as good as you thought you would, you may get fewer problems to solve than you hoped and you will be left with equipment that you really can't use for anything other than Bitcoin mining.

Holding

As one of the biggest investment options for Bitcoins, holding has truly made a name for itself. The smartest Bitcoin investors are the ones who hold onto their Bitcoin. This is a process that is used in many other investing situations, but it has truly paid off for the Bitcoin investors. Holding is one of the smartest things that you can do when you invest in Bitcoins, and it is something that will allow you the chance to build the biggest profits.

As previously discussed, the people who invested in Bitcoin when it first started out and held onto their Bitcoin until now are worth millions of dollars and are able to use that money in many different ways. They can even make sure that they are getting the most out of it and that they are able to, essentially, buy anything that they want. People who deal in Bitcoins will even spell their expensive boats and homes for Bitcoin instead of ask for regular money for it. The people who have the Bitcoin are all within a community and deal with each other. Until 2013, many of them did their dealings on the silk road.

If you are going to invest in Bitcoin, it will be easiest for you to simply hold onto the Bitcoin. This is a no hassle, no maintenance way to do investing. You would simply need to buy the Bitcoin, hold onto it in your Bitcoin wallet (and not touch it to spend on things) while waiting for it to mature in value. The chances that the value will go up are high, and you will be able to get a lot of benefits from holding onto the Bitcoin.

Selling

Selling Bitcoin is the easiest way that you can make money. If you have been holding the Bitcoin for a long time or if you just want to make a small profit off of it, you need to make sure that you are able to sell it for a good price. The price that you sell it for should be higher than the price that you purchased it for. While it may be unrealistic to expect that you are going to be able to sell it for anywhere even near 200% of the price that you paid for it, you should make sure that you are getting, at least, a small profit off of it.

When you have held onto your Bitcoin for a long time, the choice can be tricky to sell it. You may want to hold onto it for even longer so that you can make more profit on it. The easy way to do this is to only sell a *portion* of the Bitcoin instead of trying to sell all of it at one time. This will allow you to make some money off of it at the time that you want to sell it while also still having the chance to make a higher profit off of it at a later time.

If you are planning on selling it right away, you should see the average of the price in the recent past and make sure that you are selling it at the right time. The trends usually stay around the same and trying to predict when it is going to can be tricky, but it can also be very rewarding for you to make sure that you are getting the most out of it. Try to find a time when the price is high within that week and sell it then.

Merchant

You can make money as a merchant with Bitcoin. If you have a service or a product that you can offer to other people, you can sell it to them for a Bitcoin profit instead of using actual money to get paid. The benefit to this is, of course, the fact that you can make money off of the Bitcoin that you have received.

While you are able to make money off of a dollar, or real money, it can be harder to do so or take a long time to be able to make the money that you want.

By offering your product or service and asking people to pay you in Bitcoin, you are giving yourself a chance to grow the money with the rising value of Bitcoin. It will allow you a chance to make sure that you are making more money with it because the Bitcoin value is expected to rise in the coming years. For example, if you charge someone $900 for a completed portfolio redesign, you can ask them to pay you 1 Bitcoin instead. When they pay you that and it goes into your wallet, it will be able to sit there. In a few months, if the value goes up, you can sell the Bitcoin for $1,200 or whatever the value of the Bitcoin is then.

The biggest problem with this is if, in a rare twist of events, the value of the Bitcoin goes down instead of going up. This could cause you to lose money and would be detrimental to your ability to make money. You will likely lose money, and that can be a problem especially if this is the only way that you get paid. It is important to evaluate the risk that is associated with it and make sure that your payments are really worth that risk.

Day Trading

Similar to selling immediately after you get Bitcoin, you can also day trade. This is the act of getting Bitcoin and selling it immediately after you have gotten it. It all happens between the opening and the closing of a day, and you can take advantage of the lowest and the highest average prices for that day. When you choose to day trade, you may not get the best return on your investment over a long period of time, but you will be able to get a lot of smaller returns on the little investments that you make.

To day trade, you will need to find the lowest price on the day. That is the time when you purchase your Bitcoin. Say, for example, that the lowest price for the day was $913. You could purchase your Bitcoin at that point and only need to spend $913 on it. You would then need to keep track of the rest of the prices and see what the highest one was. The highest price could be something like $933. You would then be able to sell your Bitcoin at that point and make $20 off of it.

The more Bitcoin that you have to sell and to buy, the more you will be able to profit. If you have five different Bitcoin, then you would have been able to make $100 per day if you were making a $20 profit on each of them. While this may not seem like a lot of money, it will build up over the course of a week or even a month. You will be able to make a decent amount of money even with low returns. As the prices drop throughout the day, you could repurchase the same Bitcoin and be able to make even more money from them. One major positive aspect of this is even if the prices drop significantly, you will be able to make sure that you are still profiting from the drops.

Whether you have heard of Bitcoin before, own one or fewer Bitcoins or plan to make a lot of money, you can benefit from all of these different things. It is a good idea to make sure that you are following all of the advice in this book and that you are trying your best to make sure that you are making money.

Bitcoin investing can be very risky, so you always need to make sure that you assess the risks that are associated with it. If you pay, for example, $900 for a single Bitcoin, is that an amount of money that you are able to afford to lose?

CONCLUSION

Thank for making it through to the end of this book, let's hope it was informative and able to provide you with all of the tools you need to achieve your goals whatever they may be.

The next step is to head over to your favorite Bitcoin website and buy as many Bitcoins as you can afford right now. Get in on the Bitcoin action before they go up even further in price and you cannot afford them at all.

Finally, if you found this book useful in any way, a review on Amazon is always appreciated!

DESCRIPTION

The simple term of Bitcoin can be intimidating to some people, especially those who have never purchased a Bitcoin or have ever dealt in the currency before. There are many options when it comes to Bitcoin, and you need to make sure that you are getting the most out of the investment process.

Anyone who is considering investing in Bitcoin should take their time and learn as much about it as possible. The actual act of purchasing a Bitcoin can be lengthy and can cost you a lot of money so make sure that you are as well informed as possible. As one of the best and most mysterious investment opportunities, learn more about Bitcoin.

Read on to learn more about what Bitcoin is, the way that it works to make people money from it and how you can make your own money for it.

www.ingramcontent.com/pod-product-compliance
Lightning Source LLC
Chambersburg PA
CBHW071359050326
40689CB00010B/1702